Dennis,
Remember to
look within...
& Enjoy Scott

REVEALED

Personal Visions of Transformation and Discovery

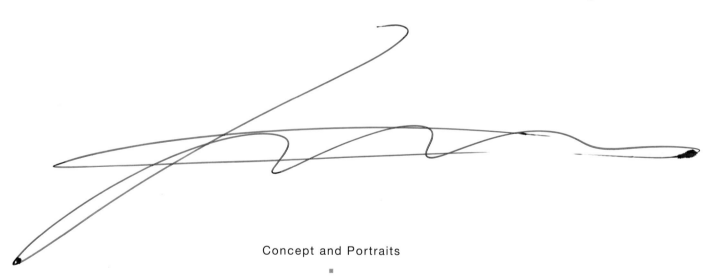

Concept and Portraits

Scott Indermaur

REVEALED PRESS

Being REVEALED

The premise of REVEALED is seemingly simple: you're given a box to decorate in a way that expresses your soul and then you're photographed in a darkened room with that box. When I first opened this book, I expected to see some interesting photos; however, what I didn't expect was the profound and moving experience I had looking at these images.

■

After reading REVEALED for the first time, I found myself sitting outdoors in the very early morning hours. There was a vast expanse of stars shimmering overhead; they looked so close that I could almost taste them. A hushed silence draped over the land. It was as if the earth was slowly exhaling… and my connection to Spirit seemed more immediate, more personal.

My Cherokee ancestors cherished this hallowed time of day. They believed that at this time the connection with Spirit was the most tangible and real. I was up at this hour because I wanted to connect with the deeper energy of this remarkable book. When I delved into it earlier and focused on the photographs, each was so meaningful and heartfelt; I had wondered if any words in my introduction could do justice to the power of the images.

As I watched heat lightning illuminating the hills in the distance, I put my hand on the manuscript hoping that in the stillness the voices of the men and women in these pages could whisper how they wanted to be introduced.

I waited. Waited some more. Only the haunting sound of a whistle from a late-night train echoing through the valley punctuated the stillness. The sound ebbed and flowed as it followed the contour of the land. Then, a feeling emerged. It swirled around, embraced and enveloped me.

I knew what I wanted to say. Although words would be linear and limited compared to the panoramic experience inside these pages, I realized that each photo was a kind of visual diary that revealed far more than mere words on paper could ever tell.

Each image profoundly captured a glimpse into the depths of the essence of an individual and even granted privy to vast secrets of their soul. Sometimes the journey seemed also most too private, too intimate, but I hadn't wanted to look away. I wanted to go deeper.

Reading this book was a kind of spiritual sojourn for me because I found myself wondering if I had a box, what I would put in it? What images did I hold so sacred that I would use them to reveal myself to the world? How would I arrange those images?

As I carefully looked at the boxes—one at a time—my response was visceral and palpable. It was as if the things inside of me that had been boxed were opening—being revealed. Painful events from the past, as well as joyful ones. Revealed. Even deeper than the outer events: the evolution of the soul, touchstones to my heart, visions of the future, and windows into what can be. Revealed. Ignited by imagination, I saw an image of myself curled up nude in my box, creation waiting to be, waiting to be born, incubating. Revealed.

In no small way, this book serves as a luscious reminder of the gifts of the heart and the inner process of your journey though life. In a thoughtful way it asks each reader to reveal—if only to themselves: What is real? Who am I? Why am I here?

My musing about REVEALED was interrupted by the soft trills of bird songs. The eastern sky was rosy. A new day beginning. May your journey into and through this book bring an even deeper revealing of your soul.

Denise Linn

Paso Robles
California
2011

This book is dedicated to each and every REVEALED subject.

Your process has been my process. I am honored to have shared this experience with you. This book is also dedicated to the REVEALED fans—your emails, conversations and support over the years have truly been an inspiration.

■

I dedicate this book to my wife, Dana, and our children, Caitlin and Trueb. Thank you for your love, support and inspiration... I have experienced my life in a way I never thought possible because of you. You are everything to me.

xoxox

Thank you to my parents and sister for their on-going support, encouragement and for believing in me.

I am playing God. Not by choice, but I know I'm playing that role. My mother kept a journal underneath her nightstand. In it, she wrote letters to my father who had passed away a year or so prior to the said letters.

I was 12 when I found the journal. Flipping through the morbid pages of my mother's unrestrained emotions and dismal desolation, I stopped and read. What would you do if you read about a mother voluntarily joining her lost love once she thought that her two sons were stable enough to live their lives without the help of a mother? A mother who thought that one day her children would be old enough not to need her?

I closed the journal, tucked it back under the nightstand and remembered forever. It's nine years later and both sons have grown.

My brother, the successful one, is on his own and making a name for himself. He built a house, bought a fancy car. All on his own.

Me? I still struggle. I still need my mother. I know I could do better. I could lead a successful life and build my own home. But the longer I need my mother the longer she'll stay. What's a home without a mother?

I am playing God; I am keeping her alive.

Royce M.

Lawrence
Kansas
2006

I carry within me a deep fascination for the unseen, for that which is hidden and not evident to the naked eye. The mysteries of worlds, and universes beyond that, which we cannot truly fathom.

As a Spirit Medium, I know with absolute certainty that there is afterlife, that there is existence of powerful energy which can only be described as pure love in eternity. It is that place where all our souls seek wisdom and solace, when we lose sight of our true paths. It is a place where all our souls connect, we are all part of the powerful energy in eternity and we are all one. It is the place of our origin and our destination.

Life is an ever-changing energy from one second to the next. There is no future; there is no past. There is no time. There is only now. It is in the now that I attempt mindfulness. For that reason, I have no regrets; I only have profound faith and I try to live in a moment of peace and love.

Growing up in a Iceland, where trees were scarce, and lava fields and glaciers were in abundance. Being surrounded by rough seas and a rugged coastline, I gained deep respect for life and death. It was a home of peace, tranquility, adventure and magnificent energy, yet with constant reminders of my ancestor's hard lives.

The symbols in my box represent life and death and the beauty of that ever-evolving cycle. They represent toughness and fragility of life. The compass is a symbol of my direction in life: always knowing where home is, always knowing that I am in the right place at the right time for the right reason, having a profound experience.

I am deeply touched by the evolution of souls and the wisdom of eternity.

Sirry B.

Providence
Rhode Island
2010

I wanted my box empty because my life is empty. I don't have anything
left to put in it. I wanted my box to be collapsed because I lost everyone and
everything in my life that meant something to me. I have little hope.

After feeling how empty the box was, I started to have some hope and
I wanted to find a way to put the box together again. To refill it with new things
and people in my life.

After this photo shoot, I have found a new direction, a new spark.

Touching the box had a profound effect on me, making me look into myself for
a new person and items to fill the box with.

Elmer P.

Lawrence
Kansas
2006

Flight: One who separates themselves from the physical body and enters a spiritual journey into the universe.

Staci B.

Lawrence
Kansas
2006

The Buddha has a smile because the Buddha has just realized he already had
what he had been searching for all these years.

Steve A.

Lawrence
Kansas
2006

Over time, I learned to recognize and trust my spirit,
intuitively guiding me beyond my shattered
and fragmented self into my poet soul.

Annie S.

Lawrence
Kansas
2006

Harmony resides in me; my spirit is lifted and the
shadows of doubt and fear are removed. I have begun
my physical healing and spiritual awakening...

Shae H.

Lawrence
Kansas
2006

Indeed I've been blessed and plan to
continue until the good Lord calls me.

Peggy L.

East Greenwich
Rhode Island
2008

I look at my box and the time
period I have captured in it as
the most profound things in life.

Frank D.

New York City
New York
2006

I submerge myself in spirituality for those I love;
I strive for genuine kindness in hopes those around
me are exposed to the deep levels of God.

Sonja S.

Kansas City
Missouri
2006

There is a higher power,
a god of my understanding.

Spencer B.

Lincoln
Rhode Island
2008

Happening is the name of the most spiritual and uplifting experience of my life. Twice a year, about twenty high schoolers sign up for a weekend conference they know nothing about. And twice a year, about twenty high schoolers leave, changed forever.

In October of 2005, I was one of those changed high schoolers. I learned to believe in spirit and self and love. I entered the weekend having no expectations and no idea what I was in for; I left crying and never wanting to leave. Back in school on Monday, I seemed bubbly and better-than-ever. I wanted so much for everyone to feel a piece of what I was feeling, but whenever I tried to explain what I'd been through that weekend, people would say "Oh that's nice," and go back to their everyday lives.

I wanted to scream and tell them that my life was changed and I was in love! But the second I started explaining that *Happening* was a "spiritual experience," my friends would roll their eyes and say I was in a cult. "Lay off the blue juice," they said. I laughed it off, but inside I was absolutely crushed. Knowing that they didn't want to hear about the best weekend of my life hurt more than I imagined.

I can honestly say that I have never laughed as much, smiled as much, and cried as much as I did those two days. When I say it out loud, it sounds so fake, like the weekend was a surreal out-of-body experience. But *Happening* isn't just about the weekend, it's about taking the weekend out into the "real world" and spreading the light that shines within you. *Happening* is the place where I found my light. I learned to trust. I learned to love. I learned to be myself without worrying about what other people thought. *Happening* is the only place where I have ever been myself completely, with no masks to hide behind. It's the only place I've ever dropped my inhibitions and insecurities and let everyone around me see my "true self."

Even now, finding words to describe *Happening* seems impossible. It's a melting pot of emotions and a real life-changing experience. Until that weekend, I didn't know it was possible to feel so much feeling. I've never been so blinded by love about anything or anyone, but the love I feel for those people and that weekend is greater than any other kind of love I know. Because of *Happening*, I believe in spirit and love. *Happening* was my catalyst. What's yours?

Marissa H.

Lincoln
Rhode Island
2008

As a single guy whose only child has left the nest, Calico is my dearest companion. She came to me last September as a 5-week-old kitten when some unknown person abandoned her on the side of a busy highway. There she sat, for God knows how long until, long after dark, I came speeding by and, for a split second saw... something... in my headlights.

Consider, if you will, how incredibly wise the survival instinct was in this 5-week-old kitten. If her instinct had told her to stand in the middle of the highway and cry for help, she wouldn't have lasted a minute. If her instinct had told her to run from the hideous noises and fumes and hide in the tall grass, the coyotes would have seen to it that she wouldn't have lasted the night. Instead, her deepest and wisest part instructed her to stay right where she was, not to succumb to fear and run—but neither to succumb to self-pity and insist on being rescued. Just sit. And trust.

And so, as fearsome mechanical beast after beast bellowed death threats at her from mere inches away, she held her ground, waiting patiently for someone to pay attention and manifest compassion. When I drove back and parked near her, she came running toward me. I think her exact words as she leapt into my car were, "It's about time you showed up!"

For me, Calico is the embodiment of courage and wisdom. She challenges me to be so centered that I instinctively respond to adversity from my deepest and wisest part. She models for me the traits I most seek—beauty, passion and integrity. She lives in the moment; indeed, she knows no place but the moment. This is the place where split-second decisions are made that decide who we really are, where risks are very real, where rewards are beyond anything we had previously imagined. This is the place where Calico sits, patiently waiting for me to pay attention, manifest compassion, and come play.

Larry C.

Lawrence
Kansas
2006

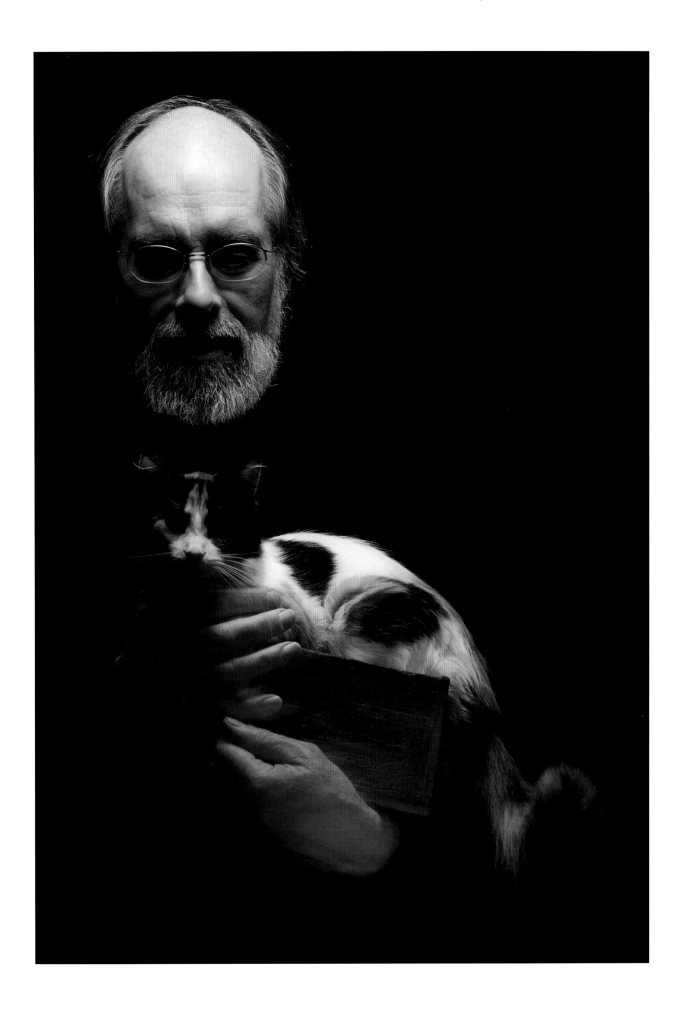

La Paloma, the dove...

She is teaching me a language of love, peace, compassion, grace, imperfection and acceptance.

It is a language so powerful, beautiful and expansive it creates wings in the expression and cannot be contained in a box.

Jen T.

Lawrence
Kansas
2006

Nature's guiding force moves me to create good through the spirits of
my youth, the Boy Scout Law, and enlightenment lit by the many bulbs
of the GE sign over Edison's empire. My restless spirit overflows
the box, measuring the infinite.

Bill W.

Lawrence
Kansas
2006

Writings, music, yarn and cotton tethers me to the Spirit and to the many lives
that entwine with mine. From these materials, I fashion who I am in this world
—writer, quilter, knitter, cantor, teacher. From these materials,
I knit myself to God and to you.

Judith G.

Lawrence
Kansas
2006

Who am I without Christ?

No one. Without Him, I am just meaningless traits. He is my Peace + my Hope.

The cross with the heart represents my relationship with Christ. The cross is made from a butterfly bush, representing new Birth + Life.

The broken glass represents my imperfections, the human part of me.
I love Christ, but I still screw up.

The nails represent the pain of life. Just because I have hope doesn't mean my life is all Rainbows + Unicorns — it's hard and will never not be hard, but now it's not bleak.

Without Christ, my "spirit self" wouldn't even be worth a picture.

Harleigh U.

Lawrence
Kansas
2007

From my favorite Tibetan Mala Beads, given to me by a yoga teacher
I adore, to my voodoo doll (my grandfather was from Louisiana),
I have run the gamut of spiritual systems.

The expression of spirituality requires a personal relationship with your
inner self; it demands the observations of your inner world and how it reflects
(or does not) your outer one.

The elekes are beads from the Yoruba religion called Ifa. Anasazi or, as they
preferred to be called, Ancestral Puebloans from the Four Corners in SW
United States and Kokopelli represent a strong spiritual connection for me, as
does the Dogon tribe of SW Mali. Apparently, I have enjoyed cliff dwelling and
the stars (the Dogon tribe knew about Sirius B before modern astronomers)
and ofttimes sense that I am from somewhere other than Earth.

The Happy "Vagabond" Buddha probably will not fit in the box, and this fits
well. This Buddha encapsulates how I feel about my life and spirituality—
it cannot be easily categorized or 'boxed in'.

In the Navajo language, Anasazi means 'ancient stranger' or 'ancient enemy'.
As I continue to live on Earth, I feel as if I have wondered through many
different representations of spirituality. Joy and the grace of heartfelt
connection comprise my view of the Tao, the way.

Quan T. C.

Kansas City
Missouri
2006

The night I decided to sign up for this photography session I had a series of nightmares.
I dreamt I was a vacant person and that I was not a spiritual person. I dreamt of having doubts,
and an empty heart, and a loss of something concrete to call my own.

My nightmares confirmed my worry that I would be judged without some label of religion,
or pathway, to call my own. In truth, I have been searching, on and off, for something to hold on to.
A religion to call my own. I was brought up to believe that religion meant spirituality and that you
could not have one without the other. I am not so sure that is true.

Here is what I know:

I find my God in nature. In the sun and in the stars. I find him at the Grand Canyon and on
a small pier overlooking a tiny lake in Wisconsin. I find him in the clean air, in rock formations,
in the center of sunflowers.

I find Oneness in yoga class. We students gather, barefoot and tired, and sit in Oneness on
our mats. I feel Oneness in my classmates, who chant, and sweat, and reach to salute the sun
together. We breathe together and bow to the teachings in soul, our teachers all around us,
and to a divine spirit.

I find Spirit in love. In weddings. In a child's love. In a cat's eyes. In a friend's hugs. I feel that love
connects us all and reminds us that we are a species that must connect.

I find Angels and Ghosts in theaters. I have felt the presence of ghosts while performing a show
and feeling a presence of an old actor in the wings. I find ancestors in personal jewelry. I have
rings from my Aunt Freda and from my grandmother, who I only knew as an infant. When I look at
them or wear them, I feel their energy. I have a sense of knowing that these women are watching
over me and protecting me. They do not judge or interfere, they just watch.

I find my Spirituality when I am alone. When I see water. When I reflect on a sunset. When I sit
in meditation or in stillness. When I pray. I also find my Spirituality in angel readings, in Tarot.
A higher force guides me through the selection of cards and they remind me that
I am not alone on my journey.

I travel with a big posse.

Ericka K.

Camarillo
California
2010

I live and breathe my passion as a plant spirit alchemist, weaving the scents of heaven and earth together for empowering the divine essence that is alive within all things.

Joan C.

Lawrence
Kansas
2006

Tibetan chimes sound. Sufi mantras abound. Sacred amulet found. Seated Buddha's in town. Hourglass sand goes down. So I ask you, Grasshopper: Who is this bearded clown?

Charles G.

Lawrence
Kansas
2006

I do not follow a dogma; it is not of my nature to be pigeon holed into one sect. I am free and I am whole by exploring and taking the best pieces from everything the human world has to offer at this moment.

Tracie D.

Kansas City
Missouri
2006

My power comes from following my heart,
passion, and instincts.

Helene D.

New York City
New York
2006

Texas, Nature and Buddha—three things that keep
me grounded and bring me peace and comfort.

Jon C.

Lawrence
Kansas
2006

Dreams have shown me where I'm headed.

Carol K.

Lawrence
Kansas
2006

I believe in handkerchiefs.

Nothing is disposable and chivalry is great.

I believe in flowers on the table, a little bud vase next to the bed. I believe in flowers and there are several poets who can tell you why. They open, slowly, to the light. They are rooted in the dirt and emerge fresh. They grow. They toil not.

I believe in art, sex, laughter, anything that helps us communicate our experience to each other beyond the ego. Communication is incredibly difficult between humans, though we seem to talk endlessly.

I believe in contemplative spirituality: meditation, practices that reconnect us with our True Self and our direct experience of the world as co-dreamers of the world. My work is about this. Through meditation practice, it is possible to experience being an integral part of a whole living world. I believe the entire universe presents itself in each one of us. I believe in holism.

I believe in treating everything as an altar and everyone as a guru, and we should bow as often as possible. We should avoid sticking out our feet toward our teachers, which means everyone.

I believe in non-belief. Belief is a fixation. In my experience, even the ground is not fixed.

I believe we give our bodies to the world as a sacred gift.
Everything we do in the world is the gift of the body.

Sarah W.

Providence
Rhode Island
2010

The Buddha, for me, is a reminder to live in the present. It's a fairly new concept for me, but is needed to control my mind and all of the negative thoughts that have started to take it over since the birth of my children. Death, disease, disasters, hurt feelings, bullying—all have a way of polluting my mind.

~ Live in the now ~

Josh T.

———————————

Providence
Rhode Island
2010

My connection to the universe is a childlike, playful feeling.

Like laughter.

And not a day goes by that I don't smile at God's mysteries, practical cosmic jokes and wicked sense of humor! I feel it in my chest, as if it has been blown wide open with gratitude. It's a moving, flowing, spinning, sensation that every single thing is in simple perfection—feeling a connection to everyone, everything. And in those moments when I'm aware of my connection, I create the most unexplainable magic, helping remind me that I too am God and that anything is possible.

Stephanie M.

New York City
New York
2006

Upper shelf: my glasses and pen represent reading and writing.
I honor the insights and knowledge received from the minds of others
through their literary expression.

I have connected deeply with family and close friends through my attempts
to share my own feelings and reflections.

The braided necklace with its four strands recalling the Four Directions,
represents the men's group work with which I am involved,
The ManKind Project.

Bob G.

Lawrence
Kansas
2006

The small fern inside the box represents my belief that in life, we are
all one with nature, and in death, we will return to nature.

The spools of thread outside the box represent my connection to those
nearest me. The spools on the inside of the box represent my connection to self.
All the spools of thread are knotted and pulled from the limbs of the fern…
illustrating the tension involved in my need to tend and mend those around me
as well as my internal struggle to understand and repair myself.

The contents define my compromise between scientific
reality and metaphysical existence.

Kimberley G.

Lawrence
Kansas
2006

Richard R.

Lawrence
Kansas
2006

The Joy is in the Journey! The Journey from sad to happy, from fool to king, from bound to freedom, from isolation to expansion, from my heart to yours. Pack a toothbrush, take a towel and look for surprises along the way.

I believe that life is never static.

It is in constant motion.

As living beings, we must accept this and keep up with the perpetual
movement that affects both the body and psyche.

No matter what happens to us, we must continue progressing forward and
stay the course. We must never stop growing and evolving, for when we do,
life stops.

What do we ultimately want when we die? To be remembered! To know that
our life had meaning? To have lived a "successful" life?

I can say that I never hesitated in my life. I never made a decision NOT to do
something because of fear or uncertainty.

Jayne P.

Lincoln
Rhode Island
2008

Jeff M.

Lincoln
Rhode Island
2008

The ash represents the physical aspect of my being.
The gold within, the light, is my spirit. My life, as I know it,
is the tapestry whose weave is influenced by these two forces.

My body enables me to experience and to be in relation to others.
This life of mine, and all comes with it, is my birthright— all the joy, pain,
desire, sadness, hope, fears, uncertainty. It's a package deal. It is my spirit
who gives this experience meaning and expands me.

There is awesome power in relationship. I believe the soul grows and thrives
on that. My box holds a photo of my daughter Mira, and her birth mother,
Mijired. This woman who lives half a world away, a woman I've never met,
changed our lives forever. Her choices left an indelible impression on my soul.
How will I leave my mark on this Earth? In whom?

My challenge in this life is to be mindful of what really matters. Can I let go
of my need for security, for ambition, the desire to control outcomes
and minimize risk?

After I draw my last breath and my soul is free again,
what will I take with me and hold dear
as my body melts away to dust?

My essence is my spirit, and my spirituality
is a reflection of that.

Sara S.

East Greenwich
Rhode Island
2010

I believe that each soul has many journeys
on which they wish to embark.

Sky P.

Camarillo
California
2010

Loving and being loved is what I care about.
It's what I believe in.

Sabine S.

New York City
New York
2006

What spirituality is to me – the love and the
connection we have with others.

Lisa S.
_____

Lincoln
Rhode Island
2008

My spirit is a child, a boy who believes in love,
truth and gentleness.

Buck
_____

Springfield
Missouri
2006

Family and friends are the most important to me
spiritually – hearts, minds and souls connect.

Paula C.
_____

Lawrence
Kansas
2007

Embrace adversity through spirituality.

Daniel F.

Lawrence
Kansas
2006

Listen.

Jennifer B.

New York City
New York
2006

It is all about perspective. See it from my perspective.

Some may try, others may not care or understand. My hearing impairment has made me who I am today. I was dealt this card at a young age and forced to make something abnormal, normal, in hopes that no one would notice. Maybe I would have taken a different route? Maybe not. Did I miss out on an important conversation? Maybe so. Do I know? Maybe this is what made me a perfectionist or helped me find the direction I want to go.

Looking back, I do feel that a higher power, God, has guided me through this journey and provided me with such a supportive family and this is why I am where I am today.

Kristen K.

Springfield
Missouri
2006

All the pleasure... all the pain.
And I have learned to embrace them both.

Martin W.

Springfield
Missouri
2006

Growing up, I had a spiritual connection/experience
whenever I stepped foot in the church. That same
experience/connection that I felt then is present today
for me through playing the piano and the beach.

They put me in a different place, a place so
much more than the physical world... difficult
often to verbalize.

Jessica G.

East Greenwich
Rhode Island
2010

I believe in a deep awareness that is within every living being.

Lara P.

Lincoln
Rhode Island
2008

All that Is, I am.

Teri W.

Lawrence
Kansas
2007

Music

The core essentials at the base of my journey are,
and have always been, largely musical.

With that perspective, the tuning fork stands to represent balance, harmony,
melody, focus and a communal rhythm of life. All of us, tuning in, breathing in
and sharing in the creative energies of the world and the world beyond.
Albeit, obvious or sublime.

A pine cone, a bird, the moon and stars, are nature.

The philosophy: The power of words and art to connect us to each other.
To our past, present and hopefully our future. Faith in the unknown,
the possibilities, and the unrealized.

Music is life. Life is music. It is a constant.

Natural, Internal, External, Eternal.

Ian C.
_____

New York City
New York
2006

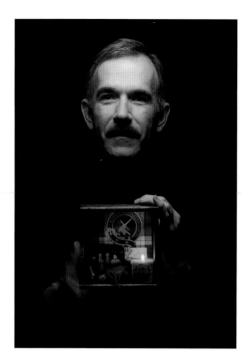

My crest bears the motto:
I learn to succor the distressed.

Kelley M.

Lawrence
Kansas
2006

I reflect your light, and like a mirror, you reflect
mine. Together we connect our souls and shine
a brighter light for all to see.

Marlene S.

Lawrence
Kansas
2006

The candle flame represents a single human life, and
how while it is lit, it glows. The flame can be blown
out, but as the matches scattered in my box show us,
there is always something there waiting to re-light our
flame and make it glow again.

Sarah H.

Lawrence
Kansas
2007

I see my path as one where I am learning to
balance body, spirit, emotion and thought.

Jody D.

Lawrence
Kansas
2006

I have found that there is only "one story" and it
reveals itself in infinite forms and plots all of which
lead to knowing "peace."

Michael F.

Lawrence
Kansas
2006

Somehow I still yearn for something as if I have
not yet arrived, like I have not been fulfilled.
I am still searching and this is my light. It leads
me through the depths of my soul-searching.

Melissa K.

Kansas City
Missouri
2006

My connection to the Divine is discerned as an inner presence...
creation whispers and awakens in me. There is a fire that fuels me with
passion for being... assuring me of my connection to the One eternal flame.

There are flowing waters originating from beyond, yet actively present and
moving through me. The movement impels me to know and to release the
essence of my being. Living waters stirring me to remember... to reveal...
and to relax into the flow.

I sense the heartbeat of creation animating and connecting me to all life...
to Infinite Presence and Mind. The life I AM is a bridge between heaven and
earth... the seen and the unseen... spirit and substance. I AM inspiration...
I am expression... I am being... I AM... singing and dancing in me.

Darlene S.

Lawrence
Kansas
2006

An instant articulate violence: excitement and tumult.
The instance of combustion, oxidation, laughter.

Rob R.

New York City
New York
2006

My motivation, my energy, my spirit, my passion, and my love
comes from God and Music.

Kelly B.

Camarillo
California
2010

All the elements are part of earth. I am part of the earth.
The earth is part of me.

Caitlin I.

Lawrence
Kansas
2006

The box represents my inner being which
contains my heart, soul and Christ-consciousness.
I am listening intently for the wisdom within.

Michelle C.

Lawrence
Kansas
2006

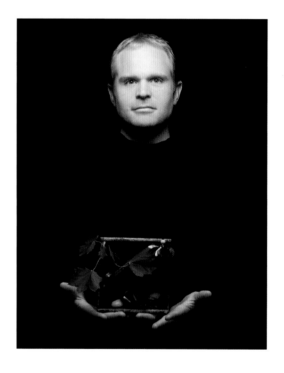

As I seek truth, I seem to discover that there
are many more questions than answers;
I am grateful for the mystery.

Corey L.

Lincoln
Rhode Island
2008

I feel close to God when I am in my garden witnessing
the miracles and the cycles of life—seeding, nurturing,
growing, fading away, resting, rebirth.

Karen M.

East Greenwich
Rhode Island
2008

Just as life burst forth from this box, our spirits burst forth. Full of life. An integral part of nature. Beautiful, Fragile, Perpetual.

Rob W.

Springfield
Missouri
2006

At any given moment, I am simply in between what I was and what I am about to become.

Mark Z.

Lawrence
Kansas
2006

It is in serving, forgiving, loving, that I meet Love. I experience God. I live a spirit-filled life.

Beth W.

Lawrence
Kansas
2006

Stephen R.

Lincoln
Rhode Island
2008

The box could not hold it all, so I brought a box of my own: a Hercules
Gunpowder Box, a fitting repository for my spirit. The plants are from my
garden, my solace, my center, my place to connect to the bounty and
wonder of the Universe. I filled my box with old wounds, many half-healed.
Even as I stand under the lights, my back aches from the car crash.

I question myself and my right to be here.

I question my creative fire.

But on top of it all is a small wooden box, carved by my brother out of a single
chunk of cedar. He carved it for me when I was young and full of boundless rage
—some of it directed at him. He carved it with love, as an act of contrition that
I did not come to fully understand until years after he had died. It is the most
precious thing I own, this box. It represents hope and compassion for
the wounded parts of me.

Being a part of the REVEALED project, I was unaware of the profound experience that I was about to embark on. The REVEALED project gave me insight on how I viewed my life. I have a very close relationship with my family and not too long prior to doing the project, I had lost my sister, Rasha, very tragically, in an accident. The feelings associated with grief—such as confusion, frustration, rage and sorrow—were trapped inside of my spiritual self all at the same time… and I was lost.

The order and placement of the objects in the REVEALED box represented the relationship I have with myself and the interests I shared with my sister Rasha. Organized and carefully placed with lots of love, the colorful objects are all part of my "happy self," but within my spiritual state there was also sadness and anger. I wanted to scream, scream from all the pain that I was feeling from losing her, but I couldn't for whatever reason. I was fearful of letting go because that would make it real. The feeling of grief and sadness scared me so much that I felt I lost the ability to scream, talk and represent her.

Once I finished the process of this project, I felt empowered. Hope and a feeling of relief came over me. The photograph captured every essence of my spiritual and emotional state that I was experiencing. Seeing it, I felt very exposed and that helped in healing a little part of my spiritual self.

Suhair S.

Lincoln
Rhode Island
2008

I choose to live in a world that acknowledges
the paradoxes, but dwells on the majesty,
the music, the marriage.

Susanna C.

Lawrence
Kansas
2006

I know my soul has potential.
It is waiting patiently to fully manifest.

Mike F.

Lawrence
Kansas
2006

New sources of life find you when you least
expect them to. When I found Elvis, he had no one.
Now because of me, he has learned again to play,
to be happy, and to be himself.

Lisa P.

Kansas City
Missouri
2006

"There must be some mistake; this is my brain, not yours."
Fikshin frowned. "Sorry," he said, "I'll just go now."
"No," I interrupted, "you can stay and keep me company.
I'm trying to find my inner self."

Ayah A.

Lawrence
Kansas
2007

I think of spirituality as a question, and I think
everything that happens can be an answer to
that question.

Sara C.

Lawrence
Kansas
2006

There is a confidence in comfort that shines through
when we are in the right place in our life journey.

Nicole C.

Lawrence
Kansas
2006

My box appears empty.

The emptiness can be seen as devoid of anything, lacking, or, in some other way,
not good enough. In many was, that is how my mind thinks of this world...
as wrong, needing to be fixed, going downhill, empty of enough people who care.

But, in these moments (which are growing in number and intensity) where my
spiritual beliefs surface into my mind and my heart, I remember that there is
enough love, enough wonder, enough beauty, enough good deeds. There is
enough. It is all there, waiting to be tapped into, waiting for our call.

I remember to be thankful before I experience it. I remember to behold the
power of mind to create exactly what it dwells on, and so to dwell on love,
peace, harmony, thankfulness, health and beauty.

I remember that the essence of my soul is love itself, and that the spark of the
divine is resting firmly inside the essence, as it is for all of us. I imagine
tapping into the invisible and manifesting the incredible.

And so, the box appears empty, but is really filled with the invisible potential
for love to come alive, over and over and over again.

Tiffany C.

Kansas City
Missouri
2006

It's been over a year since I had my photo done for this project and, for some reason, I keep putting off the essay. It occurred to me that I must be avoiding the confrontation of my own spirituality.

I've had a tumultuous relationship with spirituality, and especially religion, for as long as I can remember. My parents raised me as a Jehovah's Witness. The first chance I got, which was 2 days after I turned 18, I left that and never looked back. The concepts of God and spirituality were frightening and overwhelming, required too much work for too little reward. At that time, all I knew for certain was that I wouldn't find spirituality in the Kingdom Hall. My scientific mind needed something more logical, concrete, and visible. My artistic soul needed something less restrictive, intolerant, and unrewarding. The next 10 years were spent avoiding any form of religion, which I was raised to believe was intricately and inseparably tied to spirituality.

During that time my sister, to whom I was very close, died unexpectedly. The incident left me with a nagging need to know where she was, what had happened to her, and how I could be close to her again.

Several years later my daughter was born. In her, I glimpsed the familiar love and radiance of my sister, along with the joy of getting to know a brand new little person. I began to understand that spirituality is the endless life cycle of energy and connection. My sister could be found in my daughter, in myself, in everything I wanted her to be in. I began to understand that life has no boundaries. I realized that spirituality is not found in a building or in a book. Nor is it what one person or group tells me it is. Spirituality is whatever I want it to be, is found wherever I want to find it. It is in people and relationships; it's in the art we create and in the music we make. It is in the difference we made in someone's life by the briefest interaction—a difference we often have no idea we even made. A little bit of our spirit is left behind in everyone and everything we touch, and this is spirituality.

This is my youngest son at only a few weeks old. Right now I find spirituality in the warmth and love of my children, in the happiness and comfort of my family, in the satisfaction I get from taking care of them every day, and in the pleasure of their gratitude shown by a little kiss on the cheek or a barely perceptible "I love you" in baby-speak or a homemade bookmark given to me for Mother's Day. Later in life, this could change. The relationship I want with spirituality could become more traditional, more complicated, or more ritualistic. But for now, this is what spirituality is to me: the uncomplicated fulfillment of a deeper connection with the rhythm of life and with our Mother Earth, wherever one finds it. And right now this is all the spirituality I need.

Laura D.

Lincoln
Rhode Island
2008

Incubation.
We're always preparing for what we don't know is coming yet.
From the vantage point of the present, we look back and see moments
that define the past. What we lose sight of, as the wheels of life turn,
is every choice we make is an opportunity to reinvent ourselves.

Amber R.

Providence
Rhode Island
2010

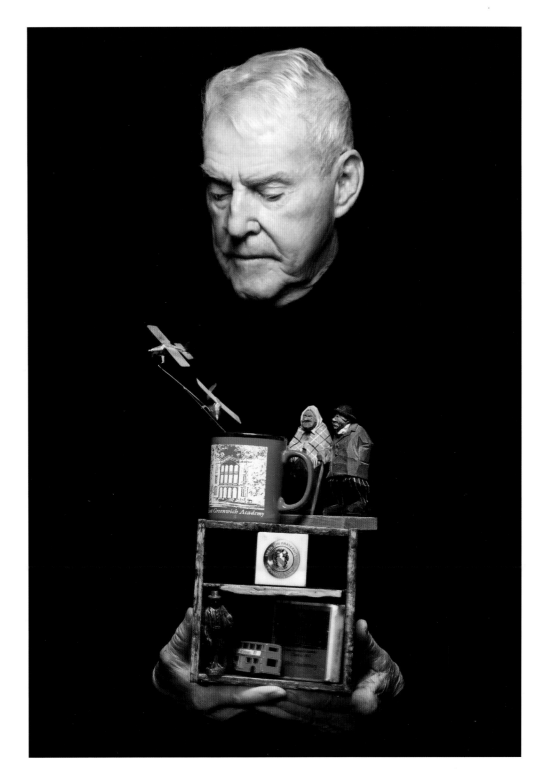

Most of my days are in the past. But maybe, just maybe, there is
some real living in the future.

Everett L.

East Greenwich
Rhode Island
2008

I chose to put a small ball of clay in my box. The clay represents a visual image that I have had of my soul... or my self for as long as I can remember. The clay, while appearing unformed, has touched my fingers and palms thousands of times. When I look closely, I can see a touch of finger print here and there— a dent made by my knuckle; a small ridge where the clay formed between my index and middle fingers... all of these light touches inform the shape of the clay.

In the same way, when I imagine the spirit essence of me, I see a shape that is constantly being refined and determined by the decisions that I make and the intentions that I have. I believe that the shape is much more affected by the thousands of seemingly inconsequential decisions I make everyday, than the few momentous life decisions. There is also a sense in me that the more I can live my life from a place of integrity with good intention—where my intentions, words and actions are in alignment—the more pleasing... or perfect the shape of my soul becomes.

I also chose to place a small prayer bowl on the box. The prayer bowl represents the mystery and joy of spirit in my life. It is also a symbol of my belief in the power of intentions... and the overriding importance of good intentions. Finally the prayer bowl was made by me... and the fact that I shaped it... with the conscious intention that, while not perfectly made, the bowl would be perfect for its use... represents the very joyful and creative realization of creation from spirit... and so it is.

James C.

Kansas City
Missouri
2006

Society has taught me many lessons and, being a good student, I have absorbed those lessons.
For years, I did more, strove to be better; I wanted the best. I set goals and reached them.
I conformed to the group. I clung desperately to the way things were "supposed to be." I was fearful
of something going wrong. I was frustrated. Asleep.

And then I woke up. (Gently awakened by the purity of my children and the beauty outside.)

Now I teeter on the edge, somewhere between knowing the truth and feeling it. I have chosen to
relinquish my false sense of control over the world and to instead control my reactions to the world.

I am letting go. I am offering up my fear and resistance to God. I trust that I will be able handle
anything that comes my way. I have faith that things are happening just as they are meant to.

I have found myself. Inspired. Alive! I will not go back to sleep.

Michelle C.

Providence
Rhode Island
2010

When I was asked to do this REVEALED project about the deepest part
of myself, I wondered, "What do people not know about me?"

Throughout my life, I have always been a fighter. Not with violence, but through
my soul. I grew up in a born again Christian family who was very extreme in
their beliefs. I broke free from the fear, brainwashing, and depression.
I became a yoga instructor, a reiki master, and angel clairvoyant because it felt
right to me. These are my beliefs, and even though I do not have a family
supporting my views, I know that this is what my soul wants.

In my box, I put thorns around the box with a flower coming out of the center.
It represents never giving in to what's around you just because you fear it.
Breaking free from the madness, growing and learning on your own.

Sarah D.

Lincoln
Rhode Island
2008

I was a child who was "born under the red flag" during the Culture Revolution. From a very young age, I came to witness the deaths of too many, including my own close-to-death events and the bereavement of my desolation. In China, to converse about the departed ones was totally foreign; you were simply expected to carry on with your life. Prisoner of my own despair, I became the architect of my heartache and learned to assemble walls to conceal the stubborn unyielding losses. While I sealed the poignant chapters behind, bits and pieces of my own self were buried among them. Life had to continue and there was no way I was to look back. I simply did not know how. There were times that I couldn't help but to speculate if there was such thing as "bad Karma" or maybe that destiny was casting a joke upon me.

I truly believe since I had observed so many deaths that they had shaped and defined who I am. There were, and always would be, times when it seemed my late loved ones were dying all over again, especially during the toughest hours of my life. I don't think I could stop missing them nor that I ever should. Nonetheless, I am no longer the hostage of my own everlasting grief and edgeless guilt. I rose through redemptions of self-forgiveness. My departed loved ones had transformed their compassion, wisdom, and love into me. Through that, we reincarnate in this life. My two beautiful children are their factual reflections on this earth. I am aware that every precious fleeting moment could be fragile, with the breathtaking splendor of life. I embody the connections: from death to life, struggle to triumph, and from the east to this west. There are teachings to be done. My children... they will discover and appreciate art in all its formations, they will learn to be thankful with what they have, they will try to give the best they possibly can, they will live with affection, kindness and simplicity in their hearts.

Erin S.

East Greenwich
Rhode Island
2010

Transformations, starting out burnt.

Jon W.

New York City
New York
2006

In recognition, there is healing.

My fears are hidden.

Tranquility in the midst of pain.

Dona L.

Lawrence
Kansas
2006

Live in the present moment, embrace what is.

Tom M.

Lincoln
Rhode Island
2008

I feel connected to the source
when I'm connected to myself, coming
from my heart space in all my
actions and interactions.

Jamie A.

New York City
New York
2006

My box is sparse and full.

There are only two items, but they are uncomfortably crammed together. A child's toy. It is ragged, a bit dirty, a little awkward. The toy is not a personal effect, it is a found and random object, but it was chosen for what it represents to me, and in me. It symbolizes vulnerability, innocence.

The barbed wire encircles the toy, it signifies strength, cynicism, and boundaries. It represents the walls that I put up to keep people at a distance, to keep them away from my insides.

My journey with spirituality is about duality and balance. Can opposite elements coexist peacefully forever? Strength and weakness. Insensitivity and innocence. Cynicism and happiness. Paralysis and possibility.

Kelsey M.
_____

Lawrence
Kansas
2006

The common thread that weaves the
many facets of my own spirituality and
spiritual growth together is heart.

Kelley H.

Lawrence
Kansas
2006

I watch in wonder as the seeds of my being
take root and grow, each containing a blue print
of life and death. Some need careful cultivation
and others none to fully express.

Cathy K.

Lawrence
Kansas
2006

Peace—my essence and my gift to the universe.

Debbie K.

Lawrence
Kansas
2006

A seed is planted...life begins... it's nurtured and fed;
twigs sprout and new leaves emerge, then blooms...
it produces another apple, the apple is eaten, the seeds
return to the ground and the whole cycle begins again
in a different spot... the past is brought to the present
and moves into future fruition.

Janeen S.

New York City
New York
2006

In hope, we see ourselves in each other where
we are comforted in the commonality that we
are all one with emotion.

Elisabeth M.

Lawrence
Kansas
2006

Family, friends and my dogs are what help
make me who I am and they bring me the
serenity and happiness in life.

Geralyn M.

Springfield
Missouri
2006

The yin-yang symbol is a traditional Chinese symbol. Many children use it when they are drawing doodles, thinking it symbolizes something close to the traditional peace symbol. In fact, the yin-yang symbolizes the way life works. The outer circle represents "everything," while the black and white shapes within the circle represent the interaction of two energies, called "yin" (black) and "yang" (white), which causes everything to happen. They are not completely black or white, just as things in life are not completely black or white, and one cannot exist without the other.

The hemp is crossed all over the face of the box, because the path through life is not as straight and as smooth as everybody would like it to be. It covers the sign saying hope, meaning the road through life takes awhile to get through, and although at times it may seem like you should give up, hope is always there; all through the ways of life, hope can be found. Even in the worst of times. Hope is a light in a dark room, that one light can seem like a million stars in the pitch of night.

Cassidy W.

Lincoln
Rhode Island
2008

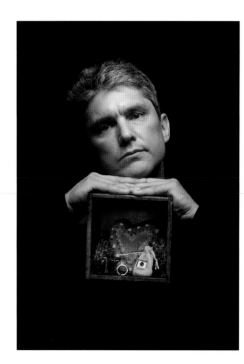

I am clear.
I am to be a channel for compassion.

David B.

Lawrence
Kansas
2006

Hummingbirds, in some way, are messengers between worlds. As such, they help shamans keep nature and spirit in balance. This inspires me to regain faith again and again.

Amanda W.

Lawrence
Kansas
2006

I receive in order to give. In that sense, creating is receiving the energy of the Universe and giving, which for me is teaching, is a giveaway of what I have received. That means living a life of conscious balance.

Ian S.

New York City
New York
2006

Much like the objects I selected, the notion that my soul is connected to spirits beyond and yet grounded to the Earth creates a juxtaposition of elements that are real and imagined.

Rose R.

Lawrence
Kansas
2006

Consciously opening my heart means it is being filled with authentic goodness, freedom, abundance, satisfaction, peace and growth. I am learning to embrace change and understand change is good.

Alice B.

Kansas City
Missouri
2006

Many lifetimes as a warrior have imprinted my soul with compassion for those less fortunate than myself, and a reminder to daily nurture my connection with the Great Spirit, whom I serve.

John M.

Lawrence
Kansas
2006

Growing up, I didn't take the opportunity to learn about my heritage
or the rich history of my people. As I get older, I find myself starving for new
knowledge of my culture and I find the views of the Oglala fascinating.
Learning the history and spirituality of the Sioux has opened my eyes
to a new world and it has given me a sense of individuality.

My box contains a dream catcher, my mother's turquoise necklace
and a book about the Sioux religion, Mitakuye Oyasin, meaning
"We are all related."

Melissa B.

Lawrence
Kansas
2006

With the birth of my daughter, my eyes were opened to see the journey of life. My mind was opened to embrace the beauty of the world. My heart was opened to the wonder of unconditional love. My spirit celebrates the Spirit for the incredible gift of Siena.

Ellen C.

Lawrence
Kansas
2006

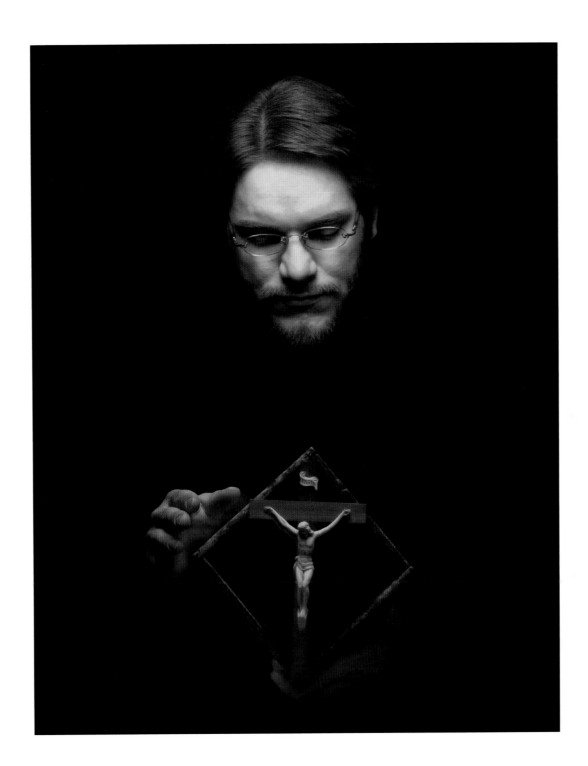

Husband, Father, Brother and Son. Teacher, Student, Laborer and Friend. Charity and Humility. Unity and Fraternity. Loyalty and Patriotism. Ethic and Tolerance. Passion and Prayer. Joy and Sacrifice. Love "For God so loved the world, He gave His only son..."

Daniel S.

Lawrence
Kansas
2007

I carry in life very few possessions, for I came into life with the most
precious gift of all, the gift of life.

My box contents contain the things that have allowed me to mold myself
into the woman that I am at this point in my journey. Red lipstick defines my
sexuality, bold... passionate... sometimes shy and blushful. And sometimes red
simplifies my broken heart that I carry in a place that is not obvious to
the human eye, but obvious to the humanity in those who have also
shared in the loss of a loved one.

Don't get me wrong, I do not dwell in loss... for there is nothing to gain
from pain, so I salute my life, my mummy, my dog, my friends, my family,
my voice, my silence, my happy, my sad, my good, my bad, my vulnerability,
my words, and my body and soul, for as a great woman once said,
"Who I am is a possibility, a possibility that's who I am!"

Tiyee C.

New York City
New York
2006

Bread, in the most basic way,
represents my spiritual path.
From working my hands through
the dough and to the air bringing it to life.
The creative force making itself evident.
I feel the immediate connection.

Suzanne B.

New York City
New York
2006

Sometimes the journey to healing
can begin only after the fire
becomes so intense
that one is burned.

James M.

Kansas City
Missouri
2006

Spirit is as individual as fingerprints. I find spiritual connection to be a sort
of thin layer above intellectual thinking and certainly far from anything physical.
It can border on an emotional feeling and can contain elements of religion
and/or belief, but I think it can also be simpler than that. I believe spirit supports
a certain level of mindful awareness that requires no effort whatsoever once
you have discovered it. It takes much effort to reach that point, of course, and
it needs constant maintenance and use, but once you have found the real
"you" and what makes you "you," you should develop and nurture your spirit
so it gives you what you need.

For me, I need to have balance in my life. No thing should ever be in excess
and all things needs to be centered towards an inner spirit, a sort of calming
happiness, and certainly a strong sense of balance. My spirit has no face,
no structure, and no name.

Good food is important to me as well as having fun.
Maybe this is my spirit's face.
Maybe this is what make me "me."

Heather W.

Lincoln
Rhode Island
2008

My mother helped me grow in life, but my father hurt me when he left.

Whitney A.

Lawrence
Kansas
2006

"So now I am glad to boast about my weaknesses,
so that the power of Christ may work through me."
— St. Paul

I find a paradox in my life, weakness becomes strength,
brokenness becomes wholeness, and inadequacies become
adequacies when they pass through His grace. Those things that
disqualified me become His tools for good.

The broken cologne bottle symbolizes my brokenness
giving off an aroma of hope and peace.

John M.

Lawrence
Kansas
2006

To everyone, a fly is quite familiar. They are always around, in your house,
outside, etc., but does anyone really know a fly? We can all see it fly around,
land briefly, and fly off again before it can get swatted away. We think we know
what a fly does, but no one really knows a fly's true life. The fly is certainly a
nuisance, but it has an agenda all its own that we know nothing about.
Maybe the fly doesn't want you to know him...
ever think about that?

Darion P.

Lawrence
Kansas
2006

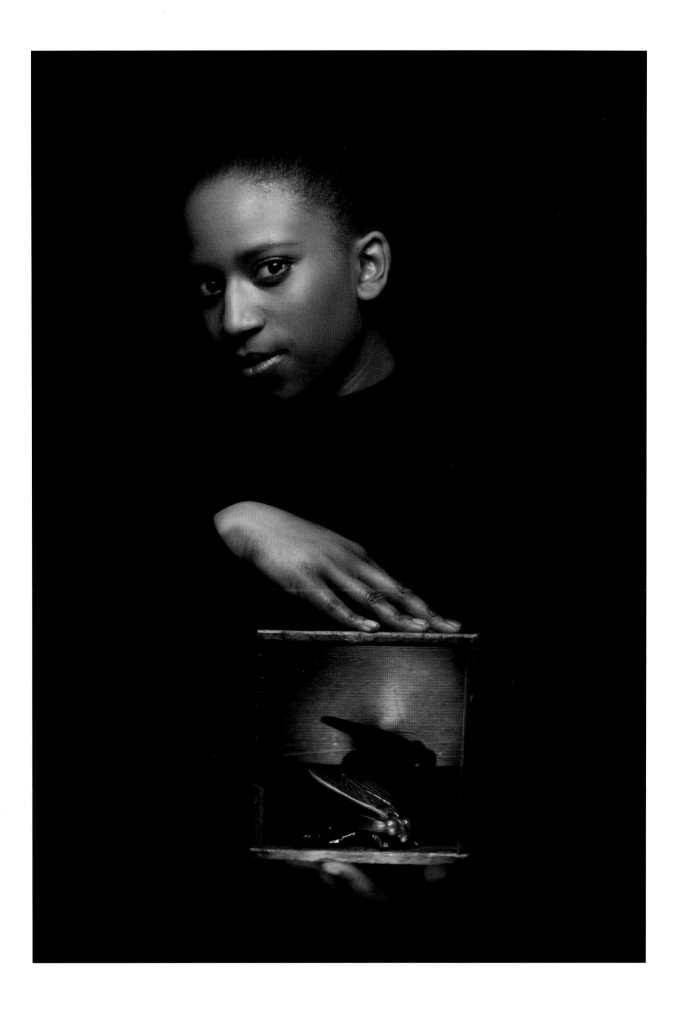

I've always had a deep connection with God. Despite being raised Catholic, my relationship with a higher being has never been tied to an organized religion. I've come to this conclusion because I've stopped going to church on a regular basis. And despite that, my spirituality has grown and has gotten better over the years. I now consider myself more of being "culturally Catholic." It's hard not to be tied to the church, one way or another, when you're Filipino.

These days, instead of going to church, I find sanctuary in more common places... or states of mind: our home's solarium in Boston, the beach where I grew up in San Francisco or just by closing my eyes and meditating. Also, I don't pray with the rosary anymore. In its place, I use prayer beads or anything close to it to be in touch with God (the non-white man with a flowing beard kind). It's liberating to not have the stereotypical image of God when you're praying, especially if you're a person of color like myself.

Another incredible spiritual capability I have is my knowing that there is something else in store for us after we die. I don't know exactly what it's going to be; I am just 110% sure that it will be incredible! Believing that our time here on earth is just a "stage" makes me want to be a better/good person. I know that whatever I do here, I will carry on to whatever is NEXT.

Bren B.

Providence
Rhode Island
2010

Psalms 23

Proverbs 3:5

In my box I place my little green Bible. This Bible sits in my living room open to Psalms 23. It is extremely tiny and only has the books of Psalms and Proverbs in it. Those two books contain the most important Bible scriptures to me; I recite them every day and apply them to my day to day tasks.

The above passages are very meaningful to me. Actually they are vital to my being. Psalms 23 is a passage that I have been familiar with since I could learn to pray. My Bible study class required that we memorize this passage as an activity. Of course, at the time, I did not realize the power of this scripture.

2004 was a traumatic year for me, who am I kidding? It was the MOST traumatic year of my life to date. Everything that could go wrong did just that: went wrong. I found myself feeling so low, abused and alone; the only way I could have possibly gone was up. However I was not alone, nor had I ever been; God was always with me. I just could not see or hear him because I had allowed myself to become so engulfed in the world society.

Ebony M.

Lawrence
Kansas
2006

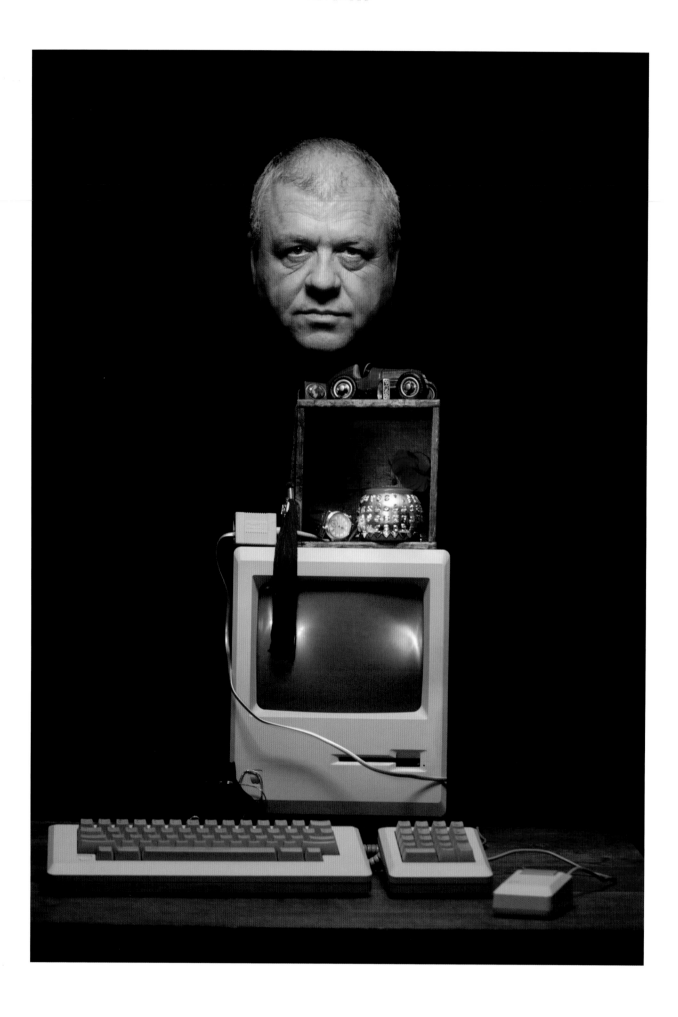

Analog is the spirit of life.
A continuous, infinite physical variable that is energy.

Birth, Death and all in between are solely the finite numerical
points known as Digital.

The journey to infinite is the reward, dark chocolate, the balance.
All, the pleasures of bittersweet.

Robert H.

Lawrence
Kansas
2006

I am living in the world that I have created for myself after 35 years of almost mindless wandering. Having always needed my inner compass to guide me here, I thought that since I have finally arrived, I would no longer need it. I realize now that I need it more than ever.

Michael V.

Kansas City
Missouri
2006

The slow steady movement of time makes the urgency hard to see.

Nick G.

Kansas City
Missouri
2006

Beauty in everything around me, even the parts we as people and a society usually ignore.

Zach B.

Lincoln
Rhode Island
2008

Shhhh... Focus, I clear my mind.
Open my heart, and my inner compass
leads me in the right direction.

Michelle W.

Springfield
Missouri
2006

My box is meant to represent the chaos in my life.

Liam S.

Lawrence
Kansas
2007

Character and style are both important elements
in defining who I am and what that looks like.
I learned that I do not allow myself to think
about my identity often enough. It was fun.

Brett D.

New York City
New
2006

I believe Spirit cannot be contained.
I believe... I've lost my marbles.

Derek I.

Lawrence
Kansas
2006

Becoming REVEALED

What I couldn't have known when I conceived REVEALED was the huge impact it would have on individuals, myself included. I am touched to learn how a simple project gave someone the gentle reminder and permission to pause from their daily grind to look within. It also amazes me how powerful this process actually is. The REVEALED subject's process also became my process. I am not alone in experiencing huge personal growth by working on REVEALED.

The REVEALED process begins when a subject commits to the project. The next step begins two weeks before the photography session when the subjects are asked to look within and find objects that represent their spirituality, what they believe in and their essence. For some, this is an easy process; for others, it is difficult as this exploration can reveal new insights into one's self and shed light on one's shadow. The actual photography session is a 90-minute process of releasing the subject from their everyday life and putting together the collected objects to represent what they have been thinking and feeling for the past two weeks. This is a progression that has brought many subjects to laughter and tears, myself included.

For years, I had been trying to figure out a meaningful photography project that I could immerse myself in. REVEALED was born from a powerful and inspired desire to photographically capture a person's spirituality. This ambition came to me as I was examining my own sense of self and spirituality and how I express these things in who I am. The concept struck me like lightning and I was immediately driven to manifest this project. As the months progressed, I sketched, wrote and discussed this idea just with my assistant and my wife. I only shared it with them because I've learned that sometimes when I share an idea with someone else, they don't seem as excited as me and this diffuses my idea and I may not act on it. I felt REVEALED was an idea I needed to build upon before sharing.

I finally decided to share it with a think tank group I participated in. The group was a source of inspiration and guidance in finding direction on many different projects. That night, I left the group very frustrated after some participants felt that this vision was basically a "terrible idea" and nobody can "capture spirituality in a box." I was told it had to be "someone praying in church or running through a field of flowers." I felt so strongly about my vision that I woke up the next day determined to channel this frustrated energy to give birth to REVEALED. What I anticipated to be a weekend project has become a significant part of who I am as a person and as a photographer. It has been almost six years since the first REVEALED weekend, and I am honored that this project continues to grow and to inspire people.

What I have learned from REVEALED is that someone else's work can also be my work. For example, when someone's REVEALED session is about their connection with their child and how much they have learned about their own life from their child's life experience, I am reminded to reflect upon my own children and our relationship. Even Royce M's REVEALED portrait and essay has reminded me to always think about my life and who I am and where I want to go.

Another lesson I learned during the first weekend of the REVEALED sessions was to release the need to control the outcome... the final portrait. As a photographer, I feel the need to manage all of the different aspects... of the photo shoot. Beyond setting up the lights, setting up the camera, and working the flashlights, I needed to let go and leave the actual experience to the subject. They were in charge of their box, their facial expressions and their hands. By casting loose this moment, I found that magic can happen—the ordinary is anything but and what is complex is usually simple... A bag of marbles opened me up to a new revelation about myself. The man who wanted to be revealed by a broken box because he felt empty and had little hope, discovered that he can put those pieces back together. This book is full of those instances, big and small, of self-revelation that allow the reader to discover more about themselves.

The REVEALED process is simple and anyone can have this experience. I ask you to take a few hours, a few days, or make it a two week process, of discovering who you are and what you believe in. Define your spirituality. Then take it a step further. Find items in your world that represent these emotions and beliefs that you have discovered. You might work alone or you might want to find an accountability partner and, in two weeks, sit down and discuss your spiritual exploration. Reveal yourself. Enjoy your journey.

Scott Indermaur

East Greenwich
Rhode Island
2011

Kickstarter Funders

A4 Architecture /
Ross Cann, AIA

Alice Ong

Blaze Schwaller

The Boyd Family

Cap and Kitty Gray

Chris Clancy

Clark Dever and Amber Rampino

Dad and Peg Indermaur

Dan, Kim, Joe and Catie Gronniger

Dean A. deTonnancourt

Designated Editor

Diane and Jet

G. Spencer Berger

Gabriel Abella

The Gerlach Family

The Hawthorne Family

Jack Gorfien

Janeen A. Sarlin

Jayne Pawasauskas

Jeff and Saba Michaud

The Jenn Lee Group

Jennifer Burland and Rob Reese

Jennifer Tábuas Devorak

Jeremy and Cherise Anderson

Jim and Tiffany Crabtree

JoAnne C. Camara

John Larsen

Karen Ortiz

Kelly and Bob Lallo and Family

Kim Schertz

Laurie Bornstein

Lisa

Lynn and Nate Rockwell in memory of Steve

Marlene Sohl

Michael and Valerie Wehrenberg

The Mueller Family

R. Jim Stahl and Mary Jane Sorrentino

Rebecca Indermaur

Rebekah Ham and Russell Carey

Dr. Rick Jardon

Ronda and Sydney Reitz

The Ryan Family

Scott and Michelle Quillin /
New England Multimedia

Selina Maitreya

Team EskimoZooKeeper

Tom and Lindsay Thornton

Tom and Mary Lynn Moser

The Wardwell Family

Zoey Stites

Scott Indermaur

NARRATIVE PHOTOGRAPHY & MULTIMEDIA

www.siphotography.com

Portraits are identified by their name and the location of each REVEALED session.
For additional information visit www.REVEALEDproject.com

REVEALED Press
East Greenwich, Rhode Island
www.REVEALEDpress.com

Book Design by Philip Hawthorne / Provoyant
Edited by Lisa Sussman

Page 2 photograph of Denise Linn by Meadow Linn
Page 124 photograph of Scott Indermaur by Caitlin Indermaur
Printed in China

ISBN 978-0-578-09837-1

With Gratitude for Your Inspiration and Support

Abigael McGuire

Allan Shoemake

Amanda Warren

Amy Wilton

Ashley Abbott

Austin Huck

Beth Burnett

Brian Shipman

Charles Sternaimolo

Chris Clancy /
Gordon's Ink

Christian de Rezendes /
Breaking Branches Pictures

Cristina M. DiChiera /
RISCA

Darce

David Fleurant

David Morris

Denise Linn

Domenica Comfort

Dona Lackey

Elizabeth Keithline

Frederic Reamer

Ginka Wandzura Poole

Gregory Tapler

Heather Wardwell

Ian Charles

Ian Summers /
Heartstorming Think Tank Team

Janeen Sarlin

Jason Dittelman /
Crestar

Jayne Pawasauskas

Jeff Barnett-Winsby

Jeff Michaud

Jessica Granatiero /
The Savory Grape Wine Shop

Joe O'Connor

John Cornelius

John Mutrux

Kathy Staab /
Jane Pickens Theater & Event Center

Kelly Balch

Kevin Black

Kim Schertz

Kimberly Gerlach

Lisa Sussman

The Mankind Project

Marianne Lee

Marlene Sohl

Maryelle O'Rourke

Meddie Reifsteck

Michael Wehrenberg

Michelle West

Nicole Purcell

Patience Allen

Paul Colliton

Paul D'Innocenzo

Philip Hawthorne

R. Jim Stahl

Ray Tudino /
Blue Line Studio

Rebecca Indermaur

Rhode Island Public Radio

Rhode Island State Council on the Arts

Rob and Peg Indermaur

Rob Levin

Robert Herrington

Rod Weiner

Ross Cann

Sarah Whitehead /
The Providence Institute for Contemplative Study
and Natural Health

Selina Maitreya

Sirry Berndsen

Staci Broski

Suzanne McDonald

Unity Church of Lawrence

Whitney Attebury

David B.

New York City
New York
2006

Joe S.

Lawrence
Kansas
2006

Jill W.

New York City
New York
2006

Na S.

New York City
New York
2006

Karen F.

Lawrence
Kansas
2006

Claudia D.

Lincoln
Rhode Island
2008